T0207657

FLYING FREE:
The Story of Kaddy Steele

By Willa Buckley Wolcott

From interviews with Kaddy Steele

To order additional copies of this book, contact:
Xlibris
844-714-8691
www.Xlibris.com
Orders@Xlibris.com

ISBN: Softcover   978-1-4134-0420-3

Print information available on the last page.

Rev. date: 11/30/2021

In loving memory
of Kaddy Steele

Who delighted, inspired, and enriched
the lives of everyone she touched.

September 5, 1917 - May 30, 2003

W.B.W

Headstrong child. Rebellious student. Excellent athlete. Aviation pioneer. Daring airshow pilot. Energetic adventurer. Enthusiastic traveler. Independent spirit. Middle East chicken farmer. Successful educator.

These are all phrases that could be used to describe Dr. Katherine Landry Steele, known to everyone as Kaddy. Well into her eighties, Kaddy remained as active as ever. She traveled throughout the United States and kept in touch with the Women Airforce Service Pilots (WASPs). This is Kaddy's life story written from her memories and told to me in a series of delightful afternoon visits during which I audiotaped our conversations.

Chapter I
Growing Up

Kaddy stood at the edge of the water, shivering in the late spring cold of northern Michigan. She and a few friends had sneaked into the area before it was officially open. The water from Lake Superior that filled The Pool, as the area was known, was usually frigid. But no one would call her chicken! Quickly she stripped down to her bathing suit hidden under her woolen clothes. She darted into the water, gasping at the cold, dunked herself until she was all wet, and raced back out. Then she and her friends put their warm clothes back on over their sopping wet bathing suits, and she took the streetcar home.

When Kaddy arrived, her mother took note of Kaddy's wet woolen clothing. "You've been swimming in The Pool," she commented, and she grounded Kaddy after school for a week. Kaddy did not really mind. She knew that summer was on the way!

It was not that Kaddy disliked the long, freezing cold winters of Marquette in northern Michigan. She enjoyed many sports from skiing, snowshoeing, and slalom-skiing to skating and sledding. Her sister Jane, who was fourteen months older, was especially good at figure skating. Kaddy, who was large, outgoing, and energetic, enjoyed all sports and was good at them all. But even though winter sports were fun, by late spring everyone was tired of winter and eager for summer to come.

After all, summer in Marquette was special. When Kaddy, who was born on September 5, 1917, was growing up, Marquette was a rather small town with a population of about 18,000. Marquette is a town located on the shores of Lake Superior far up on the Upper Peninsula of Michigan and due north of Chicago. During Kaddy's childhood, boats loaded with iron ore from the mines of the Lake Superior region stopped at Marquette and then continued on to steel mills in cities like Cleveland in Ohio or Buffalo in New York. Marquette prided itself on having good schools, and it drew teachers from all over. It also had an excellent library that was endowed for 150 years by a local citizen. Because Marquette lies so far to the north, summer days are long and typically last from four in the morning until nine at night.

Kaddy looked forward to days spent swimming in Lake Superior or at the city swimming pool, known simply as The Pool. She and Jane had been taught to swim by their father almost as soon as they could walk. During the summer Kaddy's blonde hair became almost white, and her skin tanned to a dark brown from the hours she spent outside in the sun. Lake Superior was only a three-block walk from her house, and Kaddy enjoyed swimming near Picnic Rocks, a point with four small, rocky islands that jutted into the lake. The water was very deep near some of these islands. It was viewed as a great accomplishment whenever someone managed by the age of ten to swim from Island Two to Island Four–a distance of 40 feet.

The water in Lake Superior was very cold (68 degrees was the warmest it ever got), so cold that most swimming in June took place instead at The Pool. Kaddy, like her friends, would take the streetcar to The Pool. She just had to remember to hold onto the nickel needed for the trip back home. The Pool was not like an ordinary pool. It was actually a huge, bathtub-like area five miles from the city. It was filled with water from Lake Superior that flowed in and out of ditches on either side. The water coming into the pool was frigid, but it warmed up after being held there for awhile. A long dock extended into the pool in front of the bath house with a string of rafts in front. Beginning swimmers could swim to the raft under the watchful eyes of the lifeguards. On the other side of the pool were two springboards and a high diving platform where adventurous swimmers could try a jack-knife or the swan dive. With the first sign of spring, everyone began thinking of swimming at The Pool.

Summer was also the time that Grandma Landry would come for a month-long visit. Grandma had been born in Brittany in France. She spoke French to Kaddy's father, and she had a heavy accent that sometimes made her speech difficult for the girls to understand. Whenever Kaddy asked her age, Grandma would reply, "I was 11 years old when Abraham Lincoln died." Grandma's son Jack was a professional baseball player, and Grandma, an ardent baseball fan, knew all the baseball scores and the players' names.

Grandma Landry had eight children, of whom Kaddy's father, Arthur Chester Landry, was next to the youngest. However, the grandparents' marriage was troubled. Grandfather Landry, though very likable, was a compulsive gambler. After he gambled away the salaries of his children who were working, the four older daughters said "Enough!" They talked Grandma into getting a divorce, which was unusual at the time. (In fact, Kaddy never found out about the divorce until she was in college. Then she was shocked.) Grandma and five of the older children moved far away to Portland, Oregon, at the end of World War I.

Once when she was visiting, Grandma Landry fell and broke her arm. She became very depressed, and she worried about her ties to the church. Kaddy's mother told the Monsignor of Grandma Landry's worries. One day Monsignor from the cathedral came to Kaddy's house to tell Grandma that she was worrying needlessly. A towering man, 6 feet, 8 inches tall, he arrived at the Landry home in a flowing cape and an elegant car driven by a chauffeur. To Kaddy and the neighbors peering out from behind their windows, this visit was an exciting event.

When Grandma recovered from her injury, Kaddy and her mother escorted her home on the train to Oregon. Kaddy enjoyed the adventure of the train trip. They had to change trains in Spokane, Washington, where western Native American tribes were holding a big Pow Wow. The tribes looked wonderful in their full regalia.

As long as she could remember, Kaddy had liked trains. Her father, a handsome man who always dressed in a formal suit, was a train dispatcher. He controlled the routes of trains, just as airplane controllers do today. When

Kaddy was a preschooler, she delighted in going each day to take lunch in a basket to Mr. Landry at the train depot while Jane was in school. Kaddy thought all the trains were Daddy's trains. Once when she was four, she woke early from a nap and slipped out of the house. She walked down to the station by herself and got on a train. The train had left the station before the conductor found out that Kaddy was traveling by herself. The conductor leaped off the train at the next town and frantically telegraphed Arthur Landry. After getting released from work, Mr. Landry jumped on a freight train headed in the right direction. He was very thankful to find that Kaddy was all right. Kaddy, unaware of all the worry she had caused, was thrilled to ride in the caboose of the freight train on the return trip.

Kaddy grew up traveling on trains and often went with her mother on trips. Kaddy's mother, whose maiden name was Marie Gustafson, had shown early in her life the same adventurous spirit that characterized Kaddy. Marie Gustafson had left Sweden when she was 18 after the death of her mother. Because she could not speak any English, she had arrived at Ellis Island with a tag that said "My name is Marie. Send me to Omaha, Nebraska." Marie, together with her 9-year-old brother and 6-year-old sister Amy, was planning to live with the older sister Helen in Omaha. However, Helen died of a heart attack soon after the three siblings arrived. A neighboring farm family took the boy. As Marie had to struggle to learn English and to support herself, her little sister Amy was put in an orphanage. With the help of the Lutheran Church, Marie attended an academy in Nebraska and later went to Augustana Hospital in Chicago to attend nursing school. Marie, who felt sad all her life about not having been able to keep her baby sister, stayed in touch with Amy on frequent visits. On these occasions, Kaddy would take the two-day train trip with her mother to visit Mrs. Landry's youngest sister in Omaha, Nebraska.

Because Marie Landry had attended nursing school in Chicago, she had friends in the city. She and Kaddy often took the overnight train to Chicago, where her mother's friends would care for Kaddy while Mrs. Landry shopped. Often, while Mrs. Landry was shopping for Kaddy's school clothes, the off duty nurses would take Kaddy to places like the Lincoln Park Zoo, a favorite spot.

The train trips themselves were special to Kaddy. Because she came from a train family, the porters allowed Kaddy to go up and down the train helping to make up the berths. But Kaddy sometimes got into trouble on the train trips. Once when Kaddy was eight or nine, en route to Chicago she slipped away from her mother when the train stopped in Milwaukee, and the train went on without her. The telegrapher called Mr. Landry, who was listening at the depot in Marquette. He told the telegrapher to put Kaddy on the next train to Chicago, where she arrived to find her mother waiting for her.

During another trip to Chicago, Kaddy explored the new train station, which was a huge and elegant building. It contained long benches with high backs for the travelers. Spittoons, which were large, copper, bowl-like containers for spitting or ashes, were placed on the floor at the end of the benches. Mrs. Landry ordered Kaddy to watch the luggage while she changed the tickets and to stay away from the spittoon. "That's dirty. Don't touch that," she warned.

"Okay," Kaddy answered. Still curious, she put her foot into the spittoon. When Mrs. Landry came back, a large crowd had gathered around the luggage. Kaddy's foot was stuck. All the maintenance workers tried in vain to set her free. Finally, the spittoon had to be cut off her foot, and Mrs. Landry had to pay $100, an enormous sum of money at the time. Mrs. Landry was upset!

Of course, Kaddy knew right from wrong, but she still managed to get into trouble everywhere. Sometimes she would engage in a debate with herself. "If I do that, I know I'll get whipped," she would mutter to herself. "But I really want to do it. Is it worth it? Yeah. Okay. So I'm going to do it. I'll take the whipping."

Then when her mother became upset, Kaddy would say, "Whip me then." Her mother would give Kaddy's leg a few slaps with a twig, but she really didn't want to whip her. Instead, Mrs. Landry would try to reason with Kaddy, explaining why a particular behavior was unacceptable, and asking, "Do you understand?" She would try to have Kaddy repeat back to her why Kaddy should not do something. It was not until Kaddy was an adult that she realized her mother had not really wanted to punish her.

Unlike many of the other children in Marquette, Kaddy and Jane were not bilingual. Instead, because their father spoke French and their mother spoke Swedish, English became the common language in which to communicate at home. However, Kaddy liked to hear about Sweden and its history from her mother. To entertain the girls while she ironed, Mrs. Landry would say the multiplication tables in Swedish. Then, to much laughter, she would have the girls practice the multiplication tables in Swedish. Kaddy liked saying the 5's the best.

Kaddy, unlike her sister, often got into trouble at school. She was always being compared at school to Jane, who was an excellent student. Jane had her own library card when she was in kindergarten, and she graduated from high school before she was sixteen. Jane, who was quiet, enjoyed both reading and writing and doing projects. Kaddy, by contrast, was never good at schoolwork. She had difficulty with reading, and she could not sit still and pay attention. She liked the out of doors better, and she rebelled from the start.

Some teachers were friends with Mrs. Landry, who had been a school nurse, and they tried to put up with Kaddy's rebellious behavior. However, Kaddy was often sent to the principal, whom she really liked. Since she did not like her fourth grade teacher at all, Kaddy would try hard to think of things that would make the teacher send her to the principal's office.

"Are you back again?" Mrs. O'Keefe, the principal, would ask. "Why do you keep doing this?"

Junior high was not any better. In fact, it was full of local teachers who knew what Kaddy was like. Because Marquette was a small town, word had gotten around. Even the Mother Superior at the Catholic school told Mrs. Landry that she was aware of Kaddy's reputation and would not take her.

Finally, Mrs. Landry convinced the J.D. Pierce Laboratory School with the Teacher's College to take her.

There the reading teacher worked with Kaddy but had no success. "I've tried everything," Miss Long told Kaddy's mother, "but I can't get Kaddy to read." One day when the reading teacher asked for someone to read a passage, Kaddy volunteered.

"Why have you got your hand up? You know you can't read," Miss Long said.

When Kaddy insisted, Mrs. Long asked, "When did you learn to read?"

"I think it was Thursday," Kaddy replied.

Although Kaddy really did believe she had learned to read in one day, she probably could read long before that. She would often take a different volume of the Book of Knowledge (which had only a few pictures) to bed with her. But she would not admit to anyone that she could read.

High school was just as difficult for Kaddy. For the first month of Kaddy's freshman year, Mrs. Landry would drop Kaddy at the front door, and Kaddy would enter, walk right through the building, and out the back door. It was October before Mrs. Landry found out what was going on. She happened to meet the principal on the street one day and asked how Kaddy was doing at school.

"She's not in my school," he replied.

"Of course she is. I take her and leave her there each morning," Mrs. Landry replied. The secret was out, and Kaddy had to go to school.

Kaddy didn't like the comparisons that some teachers made between Jane and herself. A question she often heard was "Why can't you be like your sister Jane?" Jane took Latin for four years and was a prize pupil. Kaddy took two years of Latin and flunked the subject.

Kaddy also had trouble with French. However, Mrs. Landry wanted Kaddy to go to college, and a foreign language was an entrance requirement at most colleges in those days. Therefore, Mrs. Landry insisted one summer that Kaddy would be tutored in French so that Kaddy could pass the exam for second-year French. Claude Lemieux, a French Canadian, was the tutor. Claude had been a lifeguard at Marquette before he started his graduate studies in Louisiana.

Kaddy would begin her lesson by going to Claude's house to have breakfast with his family, so that she could practice speaking and hearing French. Then she would read comics in the French newspaper ordered especially from Montreal. Finally, Kaddy and Claude would have a reading and writing lesson.

After the lesson they might swim from one of the beautiful, scalloped beaches of Lake Superior. One day they swam from Picnic Rocks to the lighthouse, which was a distance of two and a half miles. As they swam, they could see the ore boats. The Coast Guard did not want people so near to the boats coming into the harbor.

The Coast Guard captain called Mrs. Landry at work to complain.

"I can't do a thing about changing that," Mrs. Landry said.

That autumn Kaddy easily passed the French test. Her tutoring had been so good that she had no trouble at all with second year French. Years later when Kaddy was teaching near Marquette, she had one sixth-grade student who simply would not work. Kaddy could see herself in that child.

"He'll come around to it," Kaddy said, speaking from her own experience.

High School graduation
June 1935
Marquette, Michigan

Chapter II
Transitions

Mr. Landry died suddenly from a ruptured appendix in January, 1933. This was a severe blow to the whole family. Not only had Mr. Landry always appeared to be in good health, but he also was only 46. In addition to the grief and emotional upheaval the family faced, there were serious financial problems.

Because railroads were a necessity, Mr. Landry had been able to work throughout the Depression even though jobs were scarce. However, his salary with the railroad had been reduced. Thus, he could not both pay for life insurance and pay the mortgage for the large house he and his wife had built a few years before. As a result, he canceled his insurance, believing that once the Depression ended, he could take out a new policy. After he unexpectedly died, Mrs. Landry was left with little money with which to pay for the house. Although she went to work immediately, money was very tight.

One serious bill the family faced was to pay for coal for their furnace during the long cold winters. Because the house was on top of a steep hill, all the coal for the entire winter—eleven tons of it—needed to be delivered by September. Otherwise, the coal wagon could not make it up the hill during the winter months. (One winter, for example, 22 feet of snow fell!) Thus, the family needed to pay the coal bill of $99 in cash by September.

Mrs. Landry put any extra money into a cookie jar to save for the winter coal. Every time Jane or Kaddy would ask for something new, such as a pair of shoes, Mrs. Landry would tell them first to count the amount of money in the cookie jar. Jane would count the dollars, and Kaddy would count the change. Because there were very few ways to save money during the Depression, the sum of $99 took a long time to accumulate. Every year as September 1st drew near, Jane and Kaddy worried; they knew very well how important it was to have heat during the harsh, cold winters.

Sometimes, if the money in the cookie jar totaled over $100 by the time the coal was delivered, Mrs. Landry took the two girls out to a local restaurant for dinner. It was a thrill for them all to have the Blue Plate special, which consisted of the entree, dessert, and coffee or milk for $1.25.

Even though money was tight, Mrs. Landry insisted that Kaddy attend college once she finished high school; Jane was already an excellent student at Carleton College in Minnesota. At first, Kaddy thought she might like to become a nurse like her mother.

Instead, after graduating from high school in 1935, Kaddy went to Eastern Michigan University in Ypsilanti for her freshman year. The college was located way down at the southernmost end of the state, far from Kaddy's home. Mrs. Landry thought that Kaddy might behave better if she was far away from her friends; she did not realize that Kaddy was, in fact, the leader of many of the pranks they had gotten into.

Kaddy was very homesick, however, so she was delighted one day to spot Dr. Lee from the laboratory school she had attended in Marquette. When she called to him, Dr. Lee was surprised.

"You're not going to school here!" he exclaimed.

The college had accepted Kaddy despite her low grades in high school because she was able to pay the tuition. With so many people out of work during the Depression, few students were able to afford to enroll in college.

In college, Kaddy was faithful about attending classes, and her grades improved. In fact, she made the dean's list for both semesters of her freshman year. She had finally convinced herself that she could do the work. To her mother, who had thought all along that Kaddy was capable of doing so, Kaddy's success was clear proof.

But Kaddy had not changed entirely—she was still looking for a deal or for some way to get out of work. She especially hated writing the composition that was due every Friday. Then she met a girl from the Upper Peninsula, who was a music major and so small she had to struggle to carry her cello to and from class.

"That's a lot for you to carry," said Kaddy. "I'll make a deal with you. If you write a composition for me every Thursday, I'll carry your cello."

The arrangement worked well for awhile. But one day Kaddy's friend became sick with the flu—so sick that she missed several days of classes. Kaddy worried about her paper that was due on Friday. "Can't you get better enough to do my paper?" she implored. But the girl was too ill to do so, and Kaddy had to write her own composition. When the instructor passed it back, she commented, "This is not up to your usual standard."

Although Kaddy managed to survive her first year of college, she transferred to Michigan State University for her second year. She went to classes fairly regularly, and she held a job that paid $7 or $8 a week for spending money. One day as she was sitting in a dormitory lounge, a girl approached her. "We're looking for a bridge player. Do you want to join us?"

Kaddy became a bridge partner with a girl who was an outstanding player. They did so well together that the girl suggested to Kaddy they play other students for money. Kaddy told her that she had no extra money.

"If we lose, I'll pay it. If we win, we'll split the winnings," suggested the girl, whose parents were rather wealthy.

Kaddy agreed, and both girls went to the student union, where they played other students for minor amounts of cash per point. Together they made $25, which was far more than Kaddy earned at her job. But the partnership ended when the girl, who had spent too much time at her bridge games, flunked out of college.

At the end of the school year Kaddy again transferred to a third college, this time to Wayne State University in Detroit . Kaddy was miserable. She had never wanted to go to college in the first place and she had never wanted to stay at one after she arrived. She left Wayne State after the first semester.

Kaddy arrived home from Wayne State to find all her belongings out in the front yard. Dismayed and thunderstruck, she asked why. Her mother replied that Kaddy must either go to work or complete her college studies. With jobs scarce, Kaddy decided that she had better finish her college studies, and she enrolled at Northern Michigan University in Marquette.

It was during her senior year that Kaddy encountered her first experience with flying as part of the Civilian Pilot Training program. At first Kaddy was— uncharacteristically— reluctant to take part. The program, which Congress had authorized colleges to offer, was chiefly founded in order to get men to enlist in either the Air Corps or the Navy, thus increasing the number of pilots available in the United States in case of war. The program consisted of flying lessons and classes in navigation and aviation. When a woman challenged the right to take part in the program, Congress reluctantly agreed to allow one woman for every ten men to participate. Congress hoped that the presence of women in the program would encourage more men to enlist.

When a slot became available at Kaddy's university, Coach Hitchcock asked her if she would like to enroll. He believed that with her great athletic ability and her good coordination, she would be a natural at it.

"Why would I want to do that?" Kaddy asked.

"Don't you want to fly an airplane? I think you would enjoy it. It's going to be really exciting," the coach insisted.

Having seen only two airplanes in her life, Kaddy replied, "I don't think so. I don't think I want to do that."

"Well, think about it, and we can talk later."

Kaddy hadn't thought about it at all when the coach called her into his office.

"Are you planning on graduating in August?" he asked.

"Well, my mother is planning on it. I'm not real sure I'm going to make it," Kaddy answered.

"Well, " the coach said, "since you are two credits short of physical education, I know you're not."

"But I've been taking all kinds of P.E.!" Kaddy protested.

"You've been swimming and doing things like that. You haven't been taking the kind you can get credit for," the coach pointed out. "This program will give you two credit hours of physical education. Go check with the Registrar."

After finding that she was indeed two credits short, Kaddy agreed to enroll in the program. The coach called her at home to tell her to sign up for the required physical exam.

"She's going to take that flying course," the coach informed Kaddy's surprised mother.

Mrs. Landry became extremely upset. "You're not going to do that!" she told Kaddy.

"Yes, I am," Kaddy insisted, suddenly enthusiastic about the program. "I'm 21 years old and you're not going to stop me."

"After all I've been through, you will kill yourself," Mrs. Landry worried.

"Everybody who goes up in an airplane doesn't get killed," Kaddy said.

"Look at Amelia Earhart," Mrs. Landry pointed out, noting the famous aviator who had disappeared over the South Pacific.

"That's different."

For two weeks Mrs. Landry, at once furious and hurt that she had not been informed by Kaddy of her plans, would not speak to her daughter. Then a big Ford Tri-Motor plane made a visit to Marquette to show off the plane to the townspeople. Kaddy made a proposal to her mother.

"If you come to the airport and take a ride in the plane, and if you don't then think flying is an exciting thing to do, I will quit the program," she promised.

Mrs. Landry, who had some of Kaddy's adventurous spirit, agreed. When she got off the plane, she put her arms around Kaddy. "If I was your age, I'd do the same thing. It's just wonderful!" she exclaimed.

Not only was Mrs. Landry talking to her daughter once more, but she also was very proud when Kaddy completed the Civilian Pilot Training program and received her private pilot's license that summer.

Kaddy Steele with Instructor Sig Wilson on solo flight.
Marquette County Airport, Marquette, MI July 13, 1940
65 HP Taylorcraft Airplane
Passed Private Pilot flight test on August 23, 1940

Kaddy had one more obstacle to overcome: chemistry class. She didn't like the subject, she talked too much in the lab, and she kept breaking the glassware. At home, she turned in frustration to her sister Jane, who had recently arrived with her new master's degree.

"I'm never going to get Mother off my back," Kaddy complained. "She's always pushing me into these schools."

Jane looked at her. "Did you ever think of graduating? What do you think she's doing this for? She wants you to graduate."

"Oh...," said Kaddy, finally realizing why her mother had nagged at her so.

"Maybe I can graduate." She went to talk to her chemistry professor to see if it would be possible for her to earn a passing grade of D. That way she would manage to get a high enough overall grade point average of C to be allowed to graduate. The professor was not encouraging until Kaddy promised that she would change: she would stay quiet in class, try harder to pass the tests, and stop breaking things. Reluctantly, the professor agreed. Kaddy kept her promise, and she passed.

When it came time for Kaddy to graduate in August, 1940, Mrs. Landry bought her a new dress and a new pair of shoes. She invited a local doctor and his wife to lunch after the graduation ceremony, which was at 11 o'clock. Kaddy almost didn't make it to the ceremony. A flying lesson at 8 that morning delayed her arrival at the auditorium. The graduation march "Pomp and Circumstance" had already started when Kaddy came puffing in. With no time to waste in changing into her new dress, she rolled up the legs of the pants she was wearing, put the academic gown on over her sweatshirt, slipped into the new shoes, and jammed the mortarboard onto her head. She joined the end of the line, out of the alphabetical order in which the degrees were handed out. It was, Kaddy reasoned, better to be at the back of the line than to not be there at all. Mrs. Landry, anxiously peering around to see if Kaddy was present, was relieved to spot her daughter at last. After attending four different universities, Kaddy had graduated from college!

After the ceremony, as the graduates removed their gowns for photographs in their new outfits, Mrs. Landry urged Kaddy to show her new dress to the doctor and his wife.

"I will soon," Kaddy said. "First I have to go back inside." Mrs. Landry gave her a steely look but said nothing. Kaddy realized then that her mother knew she had graduated in a sweatshirt.

Although Kaddy was by this time very enthusiastic about flying, she knew there was nothing she could do with it as a career. Instead her mother helped her to get a teaching job in a small community called Big Bay. Many wealthy families vacationed there during the summers, and Henry Ford, the founder of Ford Motors, had helped to build a good consolidated school in the area.

Kaddy, who had hated school herself, found she enjoyed teaching the fifth and sixth graders. She liked the students and she enjoyed living near the woods around Big Bay. She met a young man who worked as a "timber cruiser," inspecting the forests, and they went duck hunting before school started. As did all the other young people from Marquette, which was 38 miles away, Kaddy went home to Marquette on weekends, and she sometimes rented a plane to "buzz" the town of Big Bay. As she flew the plane low over the rooftops of the town, everyone in Big Bay knew that it was Kaddy, and they thought she was a good sport. She was earning $1000 a year then. Part of this she spent in learning to fly with skis, as the fields where the planes landed were snowpacked during the winter.

The next year Kaddy went to Detroit to teach fifth and sixth graders in a nearby suburb for the higher salary of $1400. But the cost of living was much higher. After paying for her rented room, she often did not have enough money to eat. Walking down the street in Detroit one day, she met a friend of her parents. He offered her a job at Ford Motor Company where she would make three times her teacher's salary working on machines for the military. Kaddy declined, pointing out that she had signed a contract to teach.

One Sunday in December, 1941, she went to the Statler Hotel to have brunch with a friend. Suddenly, a wave of noise started at the front of the hotel dining room and grew louder and louder as it rumbled through the room. With astonishment and growing anger, the diners heard the news: The Japanese had bombed the U.S. Naval base Pearl Harbor in Hawaii.

Kaddy resigned from her teaching position and immediately reported to her acquaintance at the Highland Park Plant of Ford Motor Company. At Ford, she worked on a direction finder for the artillery. It was almost like a computer, but it was mechanical, rather than electronic. Her job was to test the machine. At first she was worried because math had been difficult for her in college; however, the company needed to find people who could write well, and Kaddy —despite her efforts to avoid writing compositions during her freshman year—could write well. She worked ten hours a day, seven days a week, earning considerable money for her overtime. The money helped, because Kaddy had accumulated a lot of debt after graduation especially with her purchase of a car.

Kaddy worked hard at the Ford plant until one day in February, 1943, when she received a telegram. The telegram would change her life forever.

Chapter III
In Time of War

Kaddy stared nervously at the long telegram. Telegrams usually came when some calamity had occurred. But the telegram was from Jacqueline Cochran, a well-known aviator who had won several awards, including the special Bendix Trophy, for her flying. The telegram announced that she was forming a new group called the Women's Airforce Service Pilots or WASPs. Although they would not be part of the military, they would live on an army base, and they had to obey all the army rules. Ms. Cochran said that she was contacting all women in the United States who had a pilot's license, and she appealed to their patriotism.

Without asking if Kaddy would be interested, the telegram stated bluntly, "You will report to the Statler Hotel to be interviewed on..."

"My goodness," thought Kaddy. "I'm being drafted. I've got to go." Off she went to the hotel to see the recruiter named Mrs. Sheehy.

Mrs. Sheehy showed Kaddy pictures of the planes she would be flying–the AT-6 and the BT-13. Kaddy, who had been reading about those planes, became excited. Never once had she thought she would be given the chance to fly planes like that.

"Of course, I'll do it," Kaddy thought. "If I don't go now, I'll miss the whole thing."

As it was, Kaddy turned out to be right in her premonition. Thirty-seven years would pass after the war before women would again be allowed to fly military planes.

Kaddy took the train to Sweetwater, Texas. Many other women arrived at the same time, and they all gathered at the Bluebonnet Hotel in the small Texas town.

"I wonder where we're going to live," another woman from Michigan said.

"And how are we going to get there?" others chimed in.

At that moment a vehicle pulled up. It was a large cattle car with slats across it, and with some benches installed. That would serve as their bus, as off they drove across the prairie to the army base.

Kaddy had not been on an army base before, and the austere living conditions came as a shock. Barracks were divided into bays that held six women. Two bays, or 12 women altogether, shared one bathroom. Kaddy looked around at the six iron cots with their pillows and mattresses. The walls were bare, and the floors were cement. The windows had no curtains.

Slowly Kaddy put her belongings in the footlocker at the end of the cot and hung all of her clothing in the foot-wide standing locker. She muttered a silent "Thank you" that at least her bed was on the end of one bay. That way she would not have people on both sides of her.

Then she went with the other women to get the coveralls that were being issued. Called "zoot suits," the coveralls were new and stiff. Because they were leftovers from the men, the coveralls were all size 44 and much too large. As a result, everyone had to wear them all bunched up, and they were very uncomfortable.

Finally, the women all assembled to hear the rules, of which there were many. Tightly regimented, they had to march everywhere with their squad. They were divided into two flights, Flight 1 and Flight 2. Winnie Wood, who would become a close friend of Kaddy's, was the flight leader of Flight 2. Each morning Winnie ordered the squad to line up. Next she called roll, even though, as Kaddy muttered to herself, there was no place else for them to go! Then they would march to breakfast. Afterward, they proceeded to go either to ground school or to the flight lines. At lunch time they would alternate with the other flight.

Some of the women objected to the strict regimentation, and they left the program. Kaddy, however, became used to all the formations. On weekends she joined her friends in going into the small town nearby. They had to return for the 11 P.M. curfew.

Even though the rules were annoying, Kaddy loved the flying part. The first plane she flew was a Fairchild PT-19, a single engine plane with an open cockpit. The instructor sat in the rear, and students like Kaddy sat in the front. Everyone had to wear a parachute, which was cumbersome, and a seatbelt was the only thing that held the flyers inside the plane. The plane seemed scary to Kaddy at first because it was larger than the small planes she had flown at home. It had flaps and an instrument panel, as well as very wide landing gear.

As Kaddy and her friends gained experience, the planes they flew became larger and more complex, and eventually they learned to handle multi-engine planes. Regardless of the size of the plane, the flight sessions always began with a checklist of exact procedures to be followed. The North American AT-6 was used for advanced training. Not only was its landing gear narrower than that of the PT-19–which made the At-6 harder to land—but it also was retractable, which meant that the student pilots had to learn to work the controls to pick up the gear after take-off. Although Kaddy had no trouble with the retractable gear, it was hard for some of the students to learn to handle it.

Even though all the women knew how to fly before entering the program, the instructors—all male—were sometimes impatient with the student pilots. Reluctant to have women flying, some of the male instructors did not want to give student pilots the extra time or assistance that a few women needed. As a result, many women were dropped from the program. From an entering class of 103 women, only 59 finally graduated with Kaddy.

The women who remained progressed from primary training to basic training and then to advanced training. At the end of each stage, they were given a weekend off. During one of those two free weekends during the six-month period, Kaddy and some friends had a holiday in in Abilene, Texas, where they stayed in a hotel. Compared to the barracks, it was luxury indeed!

In addition to learning to fly different planes, Kaddy and the other student pilots took courses in navigation. They were supposed to be able to fly each course with a map. They would fly over a certain area and call to the instructor on the ground, indicating where they were. That way the instructor could keep track of them. If someone didn't call in, the instructor would know that she was lost. On one trip Kaddy became confused about where she was. Looking down from the plane at the vast Texas landscape, she could not recognize the specific spot she was flying over. The scenery looked all the same.

"Where am I anyway?" she asked herself. "I don't want to get into trouble over this. I've **got** to figure out something to do."

Suddenly she saw a landing field for crop dusters with a tree at the end of the gravel runway. Nearby a man on a tractor was plowing a field.

"I could land there and find out where I am," she said to herself. Quickly she landed the plane and parked under the trees so no one flying above would spot it. She grabbed her map and ran to the man on the tractor. He sat wide-eyed and shocked at seeing a woman. What was going on?

"Where am I?" Kaddy asked.

"Don't you know where you are?"

"No, I don't. What's the name of that town over there?"

"Breckenridge, Ma'am."

"Thank you very much." Kaddy raced back to the plane. No one was standing by with a fire extinguisher as was required whenever planes took off. Kaddy fervently hoped the plane would not catch fire. Quickly she cranked up the plane, taxied, and took off over Breckenridge where she called to her instructor.

"Where have you been?" the instructor demanded. "You're tail-end Charlie. You're the last one through."

"Well, I got a little confused, but now it is all straightened out," Kaddy replied. "Sorry. No problem."

Kaddy never told anyone of her mishap, not even her closest friends. Her career would have been ended. The biggest rule (which applied to all student pilots) was that if student pilots landed at any field except their home base, they had to leave the airplane there and an army pilot would come to retrieve it. Clearly, Kaddy had broken this important rule.

The whole training period was highly regimented. Kaddy thought the women were often treated as though they were rather simple-minded, but she recognized that putting up with the treatment was a matter of surviving. She knew that the ones who survived had to be very good. Although the training period seemed to take forever, it actually lasted six months— until October.

Kaddy received her wings in a graduation ceremony on November 13, 1943. Kaddy regretted that her mother could not be there to see her, but travel was restricted–and very expensive–during war time. While waiting for the ceremony to begin, Kaddy thought back to the first review she had taken part in, shortly after they had entered the program. Then she and her friends had been put near the end of the line, as they did not have the "left-right" marching

"Kaddy" Steele WASP 43-W-7 at Avenger Field,
Sweetwater, Texas with an AT-6 advanced trainer.
Picture taken in November, 1943,
just before graduating and receiving wings.

down pat. Now they were at the head of the line. As they had no uniforms, the women wore caps, white shirts and tan pants, which the women called the "General pants" since they only put them on for special occasions. They marched in review before the generals and had their wings pinned on by Jacqueline Cochran herself.

With graduation over, the women waited for their army orders. Finally, Kaddy, along with several others, was ordered to go to an airbase in Hondo, Texas. One of the women had a car and offered to drive them to Hondo.

Jammed into the car along with their army-issue bags, the women took off. After traveling for about 100 miles, they were—to their surprise—pulled over by a state trooper, who told them that their orders had been changed to Sacramento. Back they went to their home base to pick up their new papers; then they headed out to California. At Mather Field, near Sacramento, they were told they would spend three months flying the Billy Mitchell B-25 medium bombers (the same type of plane later used in bombing Tokyo).

"They're out of their minds!" thought Kaddy as she looked at the huge planes, which seemed as large to her at the time as the big 747's of today might appear to new pilots now.

But then she remembered that each of the other types of planes she had flown had also looked scary at first. Once again, as was customary, she was given a checklist with the precise steps needed to fly the huge plane. Kaddy learned to fly the bomber aircraft in Sacramento, and she gained day-night instrument time flying from Sacramento to Ogden, Utah, and then to Douglas Air Base, Arizona. Kaddy was assigned to an air-to-ground gunnery squadron. Together with her close friends Winnie and Bayley, and with seven other women in the Sacramento group, Kaddy was assigned to Biggs Army Air Field in El Paso, Texas.

L to R, Caro Bayley and Kaddy Landry Steele
on the wing of a SBD (A-24) at Biggs Field,
El Paso, Texas. 1944

As part of the air-to-ground gunnery squadron, Kaddy took part in several dangerous training missions for the 80,000 anti-aircraft troops stationed in the Rio Grande Valley below El Paso. A major task was to fly tow-targets at both high and low altitudes. This involved towing behind her own plane a small "sleeve," which was a length of canvas about three feet wide and ten feet long, tied to a cable about 2000 feet in length. Anti-aircraft gunners on the ground practiced their shooting skills on this target. The cable inside the plane had a winch, and a man in the bomb bay of the plane would feed the sleeve out, almost like a lure on a fishing line. Wind would fill the canvas much like a windsock, and the gunners would fire at this moving target. When the training exercise was completed, the man in the bomb bay would winch, or reel, the sleeve back into the airplane so that they could show the gunners on the ground how successful they had been in hitting the target. Sometimes if the gunners shot the cable, the sleeve was gone completely, and there was nothing left to show them. Although it was dangerous work, Kaddy was confident that the gunnery leaders of the training exercise knew what they were doing.

For training purposes Kaddy would also simulate strafing the troops. That meant she would dive down at troops being trained, flying low over them. With the sun behind her, they would have a hard time seeing her. She also laid down smoke screens to cover the movements of troops being trained. She helped to train radar operators by flying over the radar equipment at night and dropping "chaff" (small bits of aluminum foil that create a snow-like effect of blips on the radar screen). After dropping the chaff, she would make another pass over the radar so the operators could gain experience at distinguishing between the moving blips of planes and the blips of the chaff.

In addition to the anti-aircraft troops at Fort Bliss, there were also about a hundred horses. Fort Bliss had been a cavalry post since the Civil War. A major in charge of the horses recruited people to ride them so they could get the exercise they needed. One of the women pilots, who enjoyed riding the horses, married the major. It was a formal wedding with a horse- drawn caisson in the procession, and Kaddy served as one of the bridesmaids for her friend. It seemed very exciting and romantic!

In December, 1944, with the end of the war in sight, Kaddy's group was de-activated so that their male instructors could be given the piloting jobs. Because the war had not yet ended, Kaddy and the other women pilots did not feel as though they had completed their job. Moreover, they received none of the benefits given to male pilots who were discharged. They received no insurance and no benefits from the G.I. Bill, which assisted male soldiers with housing and education costs. Unlike the men, the women hardly even received a thank you. No one knew who they were, and no one cared. In fact, the women had to pay their own way home. They told themselves that at least they had been given a chance to fly many different types of military planes, and they had the satisfaction of knowing they had made a difference–a major difference—in the war effort. Kaddy was thrilled with her flying experiences, and she had made friendships that would last a lifetime.

Many years would pass before the value of what Kaddy and other WASPs had accomplished would be recognized. Jacqueline Cochran worked hard in Washington to have the civilian women's service militarized—or be made an official part of the Army Air Forces–but Congress rejected that action. In fact, the secrecy that had surrounded the WASP training[1] program made it hard for the public to know how successful the WASPs had been.

After the war, efforts continued to have the WASPs recognized as veterans. Like their male counterparts, they had followed military rules and regimentation, had carried out orders, and had helped to win the war. But many members of Congress didn't want women drafted into the military, or they felt that during peace time, women shouldn't be part of the military but should instead remain at home. Some members felt that men might be left out if women were militarized[2] –that is, women might take jobs that rightfully belonged to men.

After the Civil Rights Act was passed in 1948, when women were integrated into the armed services, the WASPs were still not allowed to be commissioned as officers because they had not been militarized during the war. In 1976, when the Air Force (which had been known as the Army Air Corps until 1947) announced that women would be allowed to serve as pilots and could enter the Air Force Academy, some people hailed the idea that women would be piloting military planes for the first time. But of course that was not true. The WASPs were angry that their wartime service decades earlier had been forgotten.

Kaddy, like many of the other WASPs, felt that it was more important than ever to support militarizing the WASPs. Their stories began to appear in the newspapers and on television, and now people were far more sympathetic to their cause. The media and the public felt that the women pilots should be given their benefits for their efforts of 30 years before in World War II. But Congress was not convinced as some veterans' groups strongly opposed the effort.

Then Senator Barry Goldwater, who had served during the war at a Massachusetts airfield with more than a hundred women at his base, argued before the Senate to give the women pilots retroactive militarization. (That meant their service in World War II would count as veterans' service did.) He stressed that the WASPs were being discriminated against solely because of their gender.[3]

Although some men argued that the women had not been part of the military, former women pilots had documents showing the military orders under which they had operated and the dangerous missions they had performed. They talked of their training, their marching, and the military-style regimentation they had known on the bases.

In 1977 both the Senate and the House of Representatives voted to acknowledge the status of WASPs as veterans. As a result, in 1978—35 years after her military service—Kaddy received an honorable discharge and medals from the United States Air Force.

Republic P47D "Thunderbolt"
Engine: Pratt & Whitney R-2800 of 2300 HP
Top Speed: 433 mph   Span: 40 ft 9 in
Range: 100 Miles   Length: 36 ft 1 in
Ceiling: 40,000 feet   Height: 14 ft 2in

[1] Merryman, M. (1998). Clipped Wings: The Rise and Fall of the Women Airforce Service Pilots (WASPs) of World War II), New York Univ. Press, p.29.

[2] Merryman, p. 133.

[3] Merryman, p. 147.

Chapter IV
Is That a Woman Flying?

On a cold, stormy day in January, 1945, Kaddy was back in an airplane again, together with her friend Bayley. They had been asked by Emma, one of their colleagues in Texas, to fly her plane from Cleveland, Ohio, to Texas. The plane had been impounded, or taken over, by the government after Pearl Harbor, and now it was released to its owner. Emma called it Private Willis after a character in a Gilbert and Sullivan opera. It was tiny, seated two, and could fly no faster than 65 miles per hour.

They flew first to Springfield, Ohio, to say good-bye to Bayley's parents. The small grassy field on which they were to land was covered in snow. They had a terrible time trying to land the plane. Accustomed to bringing heavier planes in at 80 or 90 miles an hour, they tried screaming in at 60 miles per hour. The plane, which felt like a kite, would simply float across the field. First Kaddy tried. Then Bayley tried from the back seat. The men at the airport, who knew Bayley and her family, were laughing hard. "Can you help us?" Kaddy asked after they had made ten passes over the airfield. The men gave her instructions in touch-and-go landing so that she could land the airplane successfully.

Because fog covered much of the Mississippi Valley, the two women flew next to Savannah, Georgia, and then headed to Florida to visit Winnie, their friend from WASP days.

Kaddy called Emma in Texas to report they were in Miami, Florida.

"You're where?" asked Emma, astonished.

"You're not in a hurry for the plane?" Kaddy asked, and Emma said she was not. Six weeks later, Emma called them to tell them not to bring the airplane to Texas. Her husband had been transferred to Puerto Rico.

"What will I do with the plane?" Kaddy asked.

"Nothing. Just keep using Private Willis," Emma said. They did just that, letting any of the WASPs who wanted to take the plane on a trip do so.

As Kaddy needed to earn money to support herself, she used Private Willis to earn her instructor's rating. Then she was given a job as a flight instructor. She was very busy because veterans could use money provided by the GI Bill like a scholarship to learn to fly. Miami was a big aviation center, and several early aviation successes had happened in Florida. Amelia Earhart had left from Miami on her cross-ocean trip. The noted airline company Pan American was based in Miami. Miami had a huge airshow for the whole country called "Miami Air Maneuvers."

In Miami Kaddy met Jess Bristow, a barnstormer, from Houston, Texas. Barnstormers toured the country giving people rides in airplanes or putting on airshows. Barnstorming was very popular in the 1930's and 40's, largely because of the cheap cost of airplanes after the war. Many of the airplanes built during the war were put up for sale afterward, and a fighter plane could be bought for $1200. Some of the airplanes could be used for cropdusting, a process in which a plane sprayed crops from the air. Cropdusters were used in Georgia, Alabama, Mississippi, and Texas, as well as in Florida. Kaddy would go to Tennessee and ferry planes back to be made into cropdusters.

One day Jess Bristow asked Kaddy if she would like to fly a stunt plane with a 450 horsepower engine. He told her that he would like to have a woman in his airshow. Kaddy was excited.

An excellent aviation mechanic, Joe Marrs, built a motormount for the powerful engine for Kaddy's plane. Her plane was painted blue and yellow with a sunburst on the upper wing, and it was heavy and very noisy. Kaddy could turn on white smoke when she flew acrobatics. The corkscrews of smoke were important so that the spectators on the ground could see what stunts the pilots were doing. Jess Bristow knew that the crowds liked lots of loud noise and lots of smoke.

The plane was limited in the kind of acrobatics it could do because the airplane engines at that time did not run upside down. As a result, Kaddy could turn the plane upside down, but she could not remain in that position. She did slow rolls and snap rolls and loops, as well as figure eights and Cuban eights. It was a flashy show, with a flashy plane and a flashy pilot! For Kaddy it was fun–and a lot of hard work, too.

The airshow, called "World Air Shows," had five regular pilots who would travel from March to November–from Virginia, through the Carolinas, to Kentucky and Tennessee, through Mississippi, Louisiana, Arkansas, Texas, and Oklahoma. Because Jess needed to go ahead to each new town, Kaddy was assigned the duty of making sure that all the hotel bills in each town they stayed in were paid up before moving on to the next show.

Unlike most of the other performers, Kaddy had several jobs to do during each airshow. First she had to haul into the sky the parachute jumper Jack Hubert, who was the opening attraction. In the hotels where they stayed, Jack would pack the chutes carefully for the next day. Then Kaddy and Jack would fly as high as 13,000 feet. When he was ready to start his jump, Jack would get out of the plane and step onto the wing to orient himself. With a simple "bye" to Kaddy, Jack would fall over backwards. He would do a free fall without opening the parachute until the last minute. Then he would pull the cord to snap it open. He was so accurate that he could hit a mattress laid down on the ground in the middle of a circle.

Next Kaddy would do her acrobatics in the air for ten minutes or so. SNAP! ROLL! LOOP! FIGURE EIGHT! Then she would land the plane and prepare for her task of hauling a glider up into the air. She would hook onto the glider and haul it up as high as 5,000 feet, where the glider began its acrobatic stunts. At the end of the show, with the glider back on earth, Kaddy would haul the parachute jumper back up for the final performance. It was a hard day's work. But for the three years she was in airshows, she enjoyed meeting many people and having new experiences. She earned $75 a week.

It was not easy being the only woman in an airshow. Kaddy was pleased when Jess Bristow acquired a light cub plane with its wings clipped short, and Kaddy's petite friend Bayley, who could handle the clipped wing cub, joined the airshow.

Kaddy Landry Steele receiving a trophy
for aerobatic flying in an airshow.
1947-1949 (?)

During her time off, Kaddy worked as a flight instructor. "When you pull the stick back, the nose of the plane goes up," she would tell each student. "When you push it forward, the nose goes down." Compared with the air shows, this work was dull and repetitive, but it gave her some extra money.

As flight instruction did not pay well, Kaddy found another way to boost her income. First she would hitch airplane rides to the West Coast. Most pilots were delighted to have Kaddy's company because of her experience and her instructor's rating. Often inexperienced fliers themselves, they liked the idea of having someone who could help them out of trouble. Then she would ferry planes built in California back to distributors in the East.

During the three years Kaddy was flying in air shows and ferrying, her mother had developed serious eye problems and could no longer live on her own, so Kaddy moved Mrs. Landry to Florida to live with her. Kaddy worked at two jobs, running the airplane parts department for maintenance at one airport and instructing for another airport. She had so many students that she finally asked one man why they were all getting their instructors' ratings.

Kaddy was told that the Air Force was going to open a contract school in Bartow, Florida, where civilian contractors would provide basic flight instruction for the Air Force. Kaddy was enthusiastic. Maybe, she thought, if she got the job there she could remain in one place. That was important because of her mother. It was also important because of Bob Steele, whom she was dating.

At Bartow, Kaddy found out that the man in charge of flying was an old air show pilot she knew, Squeak Barnett. Squeak told her that the Air Force would not let any woman fly.

"But Squeak," Kaddy protested. "I've put six of those men through their instrument rating. I'm their instructor!"

He said, "It doesn't matter what credentials you have. They won't hire any women.

Kaddy went out to National Airlines, which was hiring men with only 300-400 hours of flying time and no work with multi engines.

Kaddy asked for a pilot's application and talked to the Director of Personnel:

"I know you're hiring because my students are coming over here and are getting hired."

"I know you are qualified," he replied, "but the public is just not ready yet to have a woman in the cockpit."

Discouraged but persistent, Kaddy went back to Bartow and asked the head of maintenance if she could be an engineer test pilot. (Every time a plane is worked on, someone has to test fly it before it is released for instructing.) He told her that he was not able to hire a woman either since it was the same Air Force. Disgusted with the roadblocks she encountered as a woman, Kaddy returned to Miami and urged Bob Steele to take the engineering test pilot position, which was paying nearly $10,000 a year.

About the same time Squeak Barnett called Kaddy and said, "If you really want a job, I'll give you one in the control tower."

As it was important for Kaddy to limit her traveling because of her mother, she accepted the job and moved her mother with her to the Bartow area of Florida. Although Mrs. Landry was apologetic, Kaddy never minded helping her at all. They got along well together as adults, and Kaddy was very grateful for all that her mother had done for her.

Kaddy had to get certified for the position in the control tower, but it was not hard to do–as a pilot, she already knew all the rules and regulations. Five months after she started, Kaddy became the chief control tower operator. Her job was to check the equipment every day. Kaddy did not mind the responsibility, and she found Squeak and the others good to work for. As a hobby, Kaddy and Bob bought a Taylor Craft plane for $600 and completely rebuilt it one winter. They rebuilt the engine, and they re-covered the wings and fuselage. After flying it, they sold it for $3,000.

In 1957, to Kaddy's great sorrow, Mrs. Landry died. There was no longer a reason to stay in that area. The husband of Kaddy's sister Jane suggested that Kaddy move to the Middle East, where he and Jane had lived for many years, and work with him in their poultry business. "But I don't know anything about chickens!" Kaddy protested.

Her brother-in-law suggested that she take a few agricultural courses.

Always ready for a new adventure, Kaddy visited the College of Agriculture at the University of Florida. The chair of the department suggested that she pursue a master's program.

"A master's!" Kaddy said. "I hardly got through my bachelor's program. And that was 18 years ago."

"Yes," he said. "But you're not the same person who got the degree 18 years ago. I am sure you must have something going for you."

Kaddy settled for a second bachelor's degree. She enrolled in a series of courses–agronomy, farm management, genetics, feeding, and soil. She sailed through them all except for genetics, which gave her more trouble because of the math. She did not know how to use a slide rule, and she had to do square roots. At 40, Kaddy was older than most of the students. The students respected her. One day in soils class, a 28-year-old student invited her to a study session. There a group of young men planned to memorize old tests to prepare for an upcoming exam.

"Are you out of your mind?" asked Kaddy. "You can't memorize for the test. You need to know how to do the soil problems." The students told her they couldn't.

In Kaddy's view students just needed some tutorial help to reinforce what they were learning in their college classes. Her own experience had shown her that she did not always have to settle for terrible grades as she had done in high school–that in fact she could do it. She knew that some students simply needed more time.

"Of course you can," Kaddy replied. She got up to the board and went through the whole problem. Then she had each student get up at the board and do the problems over and over. They were there until midnight with Kaddy doing the tutoring.

When 90 percent of the students passed, the teacher was surprised and wondered if some had cheated.

"I'm not surprised at all," Kaddy answered. "We had a study session, and I made everybody get up to the board and do the problems over and over. They're not cheating at all. They know how to do it now."

With her new Bachelor of Science in Agriculture degree behind her, Kaddy set off for Europe to pick up a car to take to Iran. Her sister would meet her in Germany, and they would travel together to Iran and Kaddy's future in chicken farming. A new adventure lay in store.

Chapter V
On the Move

When will we ever land? Kaddy thought as she paced up and down the ship's deck in the early morning. Always an enthusiastic flyer, she hated life aboard ship. But here she was, in 1959 sailing to Europe with plans to pick up a Volkswagen in Germany and meet Jane, who was flying in from Iran. They would drive the Volkswagen back to Iran. Even though she was eager for the ship to land, she was also secretly worried.

How would she get her large trunk from the Belgian seaport where the ship landed to the train station where she would catch a train to Germany? This was her first trip to Europe, and she did not speak a word of German. The trunk, stuffed with things for Jane, was very heavy.

She need not have worried, however. When the ship arrived, a passenger whom Kaddy sometimes met while walking the decks early in the morning surprised her by taking care of all the necessary arrangements. Kaddy and her trunk were whisked from the ship's dock immediately to the train station.

Kaddy's relief at getting settled onto the train did not last long. Suddenly the conductor was making her get off—with her trunk—at a long platform in the middle of the countryside. She had no idea what was happening or where she was.

"I have to do something to solve this problem," Kaddy said to herself. She recognized a few people from the ship. They smiled at her and looked at her train ticket labeled "Hanover." Their tickets had names of other places, but they grabbed Kaddy and smiled again. Finally, Kaddy realized that she simply was in the process of changing trains–that the first train she had boarded in Belgium did not go directly to Germany.

"With all those times I rode trains as a child, I should have remembered that!" she scolded herself. The ship passengers helped her drag her trunk onto the second train, where she sat silently for the next three hours, wishing desperately she could speak German. And was she hungry! She had no German money and could not buy food from the sidewalk shops at the places the train stopped. The passengers from the ship realized why Kaddy wasn't eating and gave her some of their food.

With great relief, Kaddy reached the hotel in Hanover, Germany, and put the trunk in storage. She left notes and instructions at the desk for Jane who was due to arrive on a flight from Iran. Hours went by, and there was still no Jane. What was Kaddy to do? She knew she could pick up the car the next day, but she certainly did not want to drive all the way to Iran by herself.

Discouraged and unhappy, she went to the hotel lobby to make new arrangements to go back home. As she stood at the hotel desk, she looked up, and coming down the grand staircase in the lobby was her sister Jane. Was

Kaddy thrilled to see her! Jane had been there all along, but the hotel clerks had not thought to mention her presence to Kaddy.

The women picked up their car and drove to Switzerland and then to different areas in Italy–a real vacation for them both. They spent ten days in Venice, reluctant to leave. Finally, as they sat in St. Mark's Square, Kaddy turned to Jane, "We've got to leave," Kaddy said. "We've got to leave right now."

"We don't have to leave right now."

"Yes, we do," Kaddy insisted. "If we don't leave right now, we'll never leave."

They took a boat back across the waterways of Venice to get to the car. It was nearly dark when they set out on their trip to Yugoslavia. And so their grand adventure had begun.

The only map that Kaddy had was a map from an insert in a National Geographic magazine, which showed some roads but no route numbers. After talking to different people about the best routes, they drove down the plains of Yugoslavia to Belgrade and headed for the southern plain to Nez. Planning for her future in chicken farming, Kaddy took note of the corn growing in the plain, a rare part of Europe where this occurs.

In the late 1950's the roads in Yugoslavia resembled goat paths. Kaddy and Jane had to cross some streams by simply driving through the water. Because of the language barrier, Kaddy could not ask for directions, so she would simply stick her head out of the window and say "Nez???" People would point in the right direction. After driving through Nez, they headed to the border town of Skopje. Suddenly they came to an abrupt stop. A large boat–a yacht, really–lay in the middle of a narrow road! A few cars were stopped behind it while men worked around the boat. Kaddy approached the driver of a British-made car.

"What is going on anyway?" Kaddy asked, hoping the driver would speak English.

"The yacht is too big and much too heavy to go over the bridge, so the men are shoring up the bridge to get the yacht across," he answered in English.

"But if they're re-building the bridge, we're likely to be here for months!"

"Probably," he replied.

"What is a boat doing here in the first place?" Kaddy asked.

"It belongs to Tito," he answered, naming the dictator of Yugoslavia. "It can go anywhere it wants to."

"Are they going to take it all the way to the Adriatic Sea?" Kaddy wanted to know.

"No, there's a great big inland lake nearby."

"But how long do you think it will take?"

"Who knows? We'll just have to sit here," he answered.

So Kaddy and Jane sat there, along with passengers from the other cars, and had a picnic. Finally, very late in the afternoon, the boat was moved across the bridge to a clearing near the road.

It was midnight when they drove into Skopje. Although they thought everyone would be asleep by then, the streets were packed with people

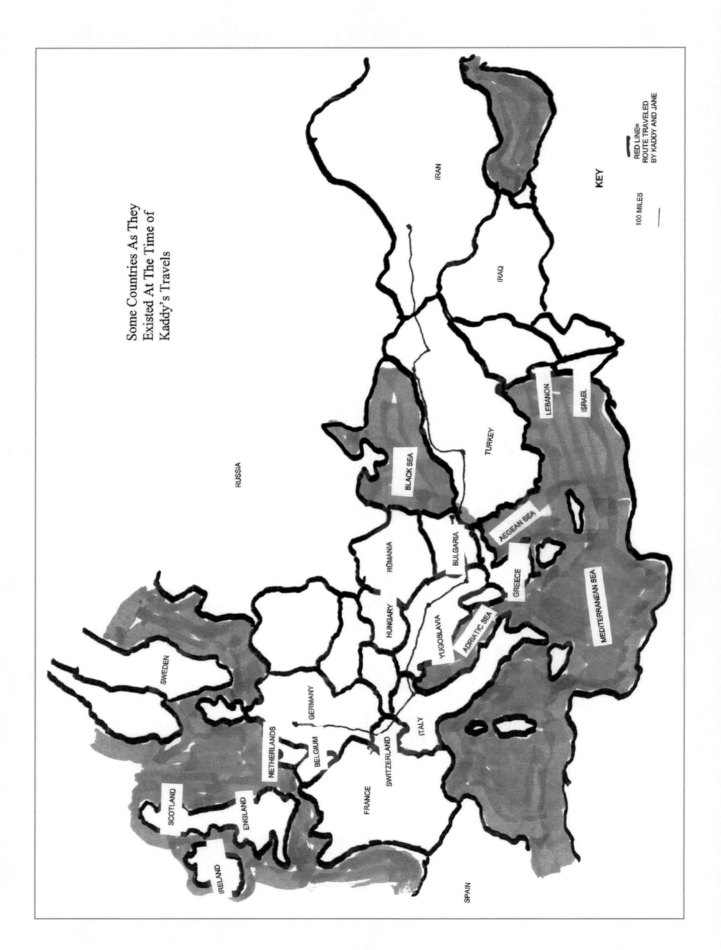

Some Countries As They Existed At The Time of Kaddy's Travels

KEY

100 MILES

RED LINE=
ROUTE TRAVELED
BY KADDY AND JANE

IRAN

IRAQ

RUSSIA

BLACK SEA

TURKEY

LEBANON

ISRAEL

AEGEAN SEA

ROMANIA

BULGARIA

GREECE

HUNGARY

YUGOSLAVIA

ADRIATIC SEA

MEDITERRANEAN SEA

SWEDEN

GERMANY

NETHERLANDS

BELGIUM

ITALY

SWITZERLAND

SCOTLAND

ENGLAND

FRANCE

IRELAND

SPAIN

celebrating. Banners hung over the street, and decorations were placed on the light poles. Clearly, a festival was going on.

They stopped at a tourist center, and Jane asked in French for a hotel room. All the rooms were taken because of the event, they were told.

"We can't sleep in the street–we need to have something," Jane told the man in the tourist center.

"We have a place that is clean and neat near the railroad yard. I'll take you there."

Off they set through the winding streets. They stopped at what looked like a warehouse.

Kaddy began to get concerned, but Jane, who had lived in the Middle East for 13 years, was not bothered at all. "Don't worry about it," she said.

At the desk the clerk asked for their passports. "You're Americans!" he exclaimed. "I'm from Rochester, New York."

"What are you doing here?" Kaddy asked in astonishment.

"A relative died and left me this business. I'm just trying to get it straightened out."

He wanted to talk with them, but Kaddy and Jane, desperate for sleep, headed for their room.

"We can talk tomorrow," Kaddy promised.

Their next destination was Istanbul, Turkey. Again there were problems getting the right kind of money, as American money was accepted by only a few banks or offices.

Istanbul was a fascinating city, and Kaddy and Jane enjoyed the days they spent there. While in the city, they met with the daughter of the late Kemel Ataturk, the founder of modern Turkey and the first president of the new republic in 1923. The daughter had learned to fly in Russia, and she was interested in meeting Kaddy.

"What in the world are you doing running around in a Volkswagen?" Ataturk's daughter asked.

"Kaddy is going to raise chickens," Jane replied. The Turkish woman shook her head in disbelief.

Kaddy dug out her National Geographic map and explained that they planned to drive across the plains of Turkey.

"I don't think so," Attaturk's daughter said. "The whole central part of Turkey has had terrible flooding. Let me talk to someone in the government and find the best way for you to go."

At the suggestion of the government official, Kaddy and Jane drove to Ankara, north to Samsun, and along the shore of the Black Sea to Trabzon, near the border with Russia. Because they needed to get their money changed again, they drove all over Trabzon to find a bank. They could not find anyone who spoke English, but after a few frustrating hours, a man came up to them and said in clear English, "Are you having a problem?"

"Yes. We need to find a bank to get some money," Kaddy said. "Your English is very good, and we haven't found many people in Turkey who can speak English."

"I'm in the shipping business. I'll take you where you need to go," the man said. He added, "There's a very nice restaurant nearby. I'll call and tell them you're coming. Turkish women never go out to eat without a man. They'll be shocked."

The evening at the restaurant was a success. They enjoyed seeing the moon rise over the Black Sea, spreading serene moonlight on the trees swaying nearby.

The next morning an unwelcome surprise awaited Kaddy. The night before she had parked right up against the building to get as far as possible off the narrow street. In the daylight she saw that the inside wheel, which she could not reach at all, had a flat tire.

Kaddy thought, "I'm not going to be able to fix this." A group of men came down the street. When Kaddy pointed to the flat tire, the men understood her problem, picked up the car, and moved it three feet into the street. Kaddy dug out the lugwrench and replaced the flat tire with the spare tire. All the men cheered!

From Trabzon, the sisters planned to drive over the mountains and down to the Central Plain. Over a road that zigzagged back and forth up the mountainside with no guard rail to protect them, the little Volkswagen made it to the pass, 8,000 feet above sea level. From there it was downhill–still a scary ride–to Erzurum.

At Erzurum a police lieutenant took their passports away from them, making Kaddy very nervous. As she went to a garage to get the flat tire repaired, a U.S. Army jeep went by. Delighted, Kaddy yelled at him to stop.

"Why didn't you let someone know you were coming?" the soldier asked. He took them to their small army base, where the lonely men were anxious to have the two American women stay and talk with them.

"We can't believe you two," the soldiers said. To everyone's surprise they found that one soldier was from the small town of Bartow, Florida, that Kaddy had so recently left!

Early the next morning the two sisters headed for the police station, where they were joined by a soldier who rode with them until they were out of the militarized zone. Then, with their passports safely tucked in their pockets, Kaddy and Jane headed east. They crossed a flat plain out of which Mt. Ararat rose like a cone nearly 17,000 feet high. (This is the spot where Noah is thought to have landed after the flood.) As they neared the mountain, they met a group of 25 Bedouins, riding camels and herding flocks of black sheep to wherever grass would be found. Although women in other towns in Turkey had paid no attention to Kaddy and Jane, these Bedouin women were delighted to see them, laughing and joking with them in sign language.

Late that evening, they crossed into Iran. With their trip almost at an end, they began the long, dusty trip over terrible roads to Teheran, the capital city. How good it was to finally arrive at Jane's home and be greeted by her family! Kaddy had done all the driving–about 6,000 miles. Kaddy enjoyed her stay in Iran, but the country was not suited for chicken farming. Because it was difficult for baby chicks or chicken feed to be shipped into Iran, Kaddy left after four months for the nearby country of Lebanon to manage the chicken farm that Jane's husband partly owned. The farm was located in the Bekka Valley, between two beautiful mountain ranges, a territory that has been rich in farmlands for centuries. Kaddy lived with an Arab family, the Macaroons, in an apartment over some shops they owned.

At first she felt isolated. She would pass the Dar, which was like a living room at the entrance to the house, and go straight to her room. The Macaroons spoke French but did not speak English, and Kaddy had not spoken French since high school.

"How are you getting along with your family?" Jane asked one day during a brief visit to Lebanon. When Kaddy explained that she had no contact with them, Jane replied,

"I don't think they like that. Mme. Macaroon is unhappy with you. She would like you to go into the Dar and be friendly."

So Kaddy did her best to join the family in the Dar. Although her French was more than a bit rusty, she remembered enough to communicate. A young boy in the family attended a French school and was learning English, and that helped. Kaddy taught the children to play poker, using as chips the dates from the family's palm trees. With the women she played backgammon.

Kaddy enjoyed her new friends, and she worked hard at the chicken farming. But when her sweetheart Bob Steele arrived from the States in 1960 to marry her, Kaddy was ready to leave. After they were married in Beirut, they bought a car and headed back toward Europe, camping along the way. For six months they wandered through Egypt, Italy, Sweden, England, France, and Germany. Bob enjoyed seeing sports car races, and Kaddy enjoyed seeing all the famous sights. When the weather turned cold, they camped in the south of France, where it was warmer. By November, it had become very cold, and they headed for home.

Kaddy and Bob settled at first on the St. John's River in Jacksonville, Florida, and Kaddy worked as a substitute teacher. After she began taking courses to brush up on her certification for teaching, a friend convinced her to enroll in a doctoral program at the University of Florida. So Kaddy, who had truly hated school many years before, found herself at nearly 50 years of age back in the classroom as a student once again. When, a few years later, she became Dr. Kaddy Steele, she reflected how proud her mother would have been!

Once she received her degree, Kaddy continued to try new things as a faculty member at the University of Florida. In the 1970's, when students of all races began attending the University, Kaddy was asked to guide the development of a teaching center and a reading and writing center. Because she well understood what a struggle school could be, she was eager to help the new minority students attending the university. A few years later, in the early 1980's when personal-size computers were brand new, Kaddy was again chosen to lead. This time she created a computer center for college faculty members who were nervous about using the new machines. To teach the faculty, she employed college students who were skilled at using the new computers. Always sympathetic to students, she trained them how to be good workers. As was the case with everyone who worked with Kaddy, the center employees respected her and liked her, and they came back to see her often after they had graduated.

Along with others, Kaddy worked to obtain recognition for the women flyers who had served during World War II. When the United States government granted official recognition–over three decades after the war had ended–Kaddy was elated. Long overdue, it was a giant step forward for women.

At the air force field in Copenhagen, Denmark

Until her death on May 30, 2003, Kaddy still remained very active. A heart attack and knee surgery did not slow her down, and she exercised vigorously every day. Although Bob did not like traveling, Kaddy continued to take airplanes around the country to see friends and to participate actively in meetings of the WASPs. She, along with other WASPs, began to receive rightful recognition, and she enjoyed the newspaper articles and radio programs that now feature the WASPs.

For Kaddy, new challenges and new directions made life exciting. A few months before her death, she received a $50 check for a story she had written.

"Since I've gotten paid for it," she said with a hearty chuckle, "I must be a writer now!" Never afraid to try something new, she proved that women can succeed as well as men in solving problems, excelling in challenging careers, and leading the way to new adventures. She showed that no one needs to be defeated by past attitudes and actions: Everyone can learn from mistakes and can turn things around. What is more, they can enjoy doing it. With courage, spirit, zest, and enthusiasm she demonstrated that a life worth living can, indeed, be a life of flying free.

Kaddy at home

Printed in the United States
by Baker & Taylor Publisher Services